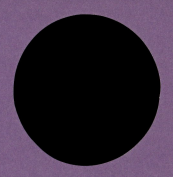

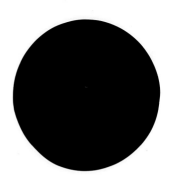

BELLY LAUGH FART JOKES for Kids

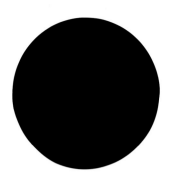

BELLY LAUGH FART JOKES for Kids

350 Hilarious Jokes for Kids

Sky Pony Press
New York

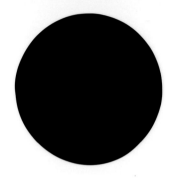

Copyright © 2018 by Skyhorse Publishing

All rights reserved. No part of this book may be reproduced in any manner without the express written consent of the publisher, except in the case of brief excerpts in critical reviews or articles. All inquiries should be addressed to Sky Pony Press, 307 West 36th Street, 11th Floor, New York, NY 10018.

Sky Pony Press books may be purchased in bulk at special discounts for sales promotion, corporate gifts, fund-raising, or educational purposes. Special editions can also be created to specifications. For details, contact the Special Sales Department, Sky Pony Press, 307 West 36th Street, 11th Floor, New York, NY 10018 or info@skyhorsepublishing.com.

Sky Pony® is a registered trademark of Skyhorse Publishing, Inc.®, a Delaware corporation.

Visit our website at www.skyponypress.com.

10 9 8 7 6 5 4 3 2 1

Manufactured in China, January 2018
This product conforms to CPSIA 2008

Library of Congress Cataloging-in-Publication Data on file.

Cover design by Kate Gardner

Print ISBN: 978-1-5107-3361-9
Ebook ISBN: 978-1-5107-3362-6

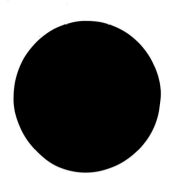

BELLY LAUGH FART JOKES for Kids

Belly Laugh Fart Jokes for Kids

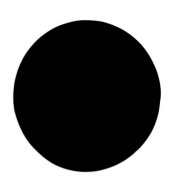

Q: What is invisible and smells of carrots?

A: A little bunny's fart.

Belly Laugh Fart Jokes for Kids

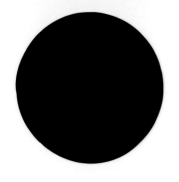

Q: **Why don't farts graduate from high school?**

A: Because they always end up getting expelled!

Q: **What's the difference between Mozart and Mr. Methane?**

A: One is music to your ear; the other is music from his rear.

Q: **Why do farts smell?**

A: For the benefit of people who are hearing impaired!

Belly Laugh Fart Jokes for Kids

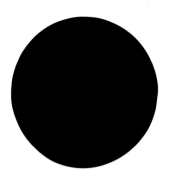

Q: Why do horses like to fart when they buck?

A: Because they can't achieve full horsepower without gas.

Q: Why don't you fart in church?

A: Because you have to sit in your pew.

Q: What did the burp say to the other burp?

A: Let's be naughty and go out the other end!

Belly Laugh Fart Jokes for Kids

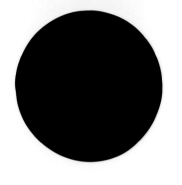

Q: When I am released to the wind, you look away and you pretend, but away your friends I will send. What am I?

A: A Fart.

Q: What do you call someone who doesn't fart in public?

A: A private tutor!

Q: What do you call a fart that smells REALLY bad?

A: An atomic bomb

Belly Laugh Fart Jokes for Kids

Q: What do you call a cat who likes to eat beans?

A: Puss n Toots.

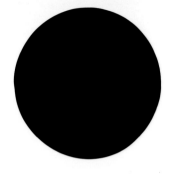

I was at a sophisticated dinner party the other day when I farted loudly. One of the guests was appalled and said indignantly, "How dare you fart in front of my wife!" I said, "I'm sorry, I didn't realize it was her turn."

A skeleton was trying to fart in a crowded place. But in the end it couldn't 'cuz it had no guts.

Farting on an elevator is wrong on so many levels.

Belly Laugh Fart Jokes for Kids

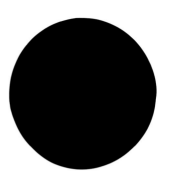

I was on the bus the other day and I really needed to fart. Luckily the music was really loud so I timed my farts with the beat, and after a couple of songs I began to feel better. As I left the bus though, I noticed everyone was staring at me in disgust. That's when I remembered I was listening to my iPod.

A boy comes home and proudly announces to his parents, "Mom, dad, the teacher asked the class a question today and I was the only one who knew the right answer!"

The parents are very happy and ask, "That's amazing Lenny! And what was the question?"

Sticking out his chest, the boy says, "Who farted?"

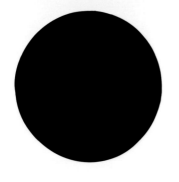

Bill Gates farted in an Apple store. He later commented, "Well it's hardly my fault they don't have any Windows . . ."

Full elevators have a different smell to children.

When people hug you, fart loudly. You'll make them feel very strong.

Mother's advice: Stop whining. Look what the couch has to endure. It has to stand every fart, and silently.

I didn't fart. My intestines just blew you a kiss.

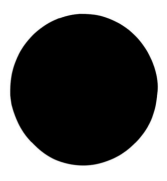

A human fart can be louder than a trombone. I discovered that at my sister's school concert.

A boy never really knows just how much he farts until he spends a day with a girl he really likes.

I was out delivering leaflets on flatulence awareness this morning. Unfortunately, I let one rip.

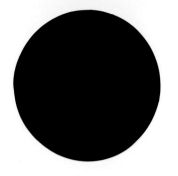

An old married couple are in church one Sunday when the woman turns to her husband and says, "I've just let out a really long, silent fart. What should I do?" The husband turned to her and said, "Replace the battery in your hearing aid."

I farted in work the other day and my boss started trying to open the window. It must have been a really bad one—we work on a submarine.

I never farted in front of my wife until we got married. I don't think the priest was too impressed.

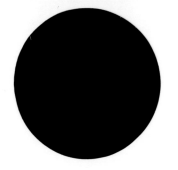

If you farted while traveling at the speed of sound would you smell it before you heard it?

I was alone in the house last night, just lying in bed, when I heard someone fart. I didn't know whether to laugh or be scared.

I silently farted in bed last night and then slowly lifted the covers. My wife shouted, "Urghh! That stinks!" It must have been a bad one—she was downstairs at the time.

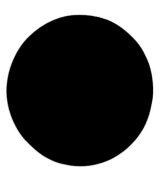

You know it's a good fart when the dog wakes up, looks at you in disgust and walks out of the room.

I made a plan to fart the other day. It's the only plan I've ever followed through with.

I went to see my doctor yesterday. I said to him, "I've got a problem with farting when I'm nervous." He said, "I know," as he finished my checkup.

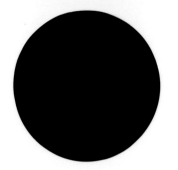

I just had a fart joke. But I blew it.

I used to tell fart jokes, till everyone told me they stunk.

What happened to the blind skunk? He fell in love with a fart.

Why fart it and waste it when you can burp and taste?

Laugh and the world laughs with you; fart and they'll stop laughing.

What Kind of Farter Are You?

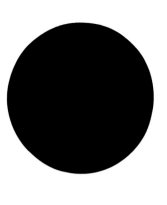

Vain: You love the smell of your own farts.

Amiable: You love the smell of other people's farts.

Proud: You think your farts are exceptionally fine.

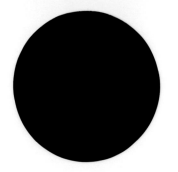

Impudent: You boldly fart out loud and then laugh.

Scientific: You fart regularly but you're concerned about pollution.

Nervous: You stop in the middle of your fart.

Honest: You admit that you farted but offer good medical reasons.

Dishonest: You fart and then blame the dog.

Foolish: You suppress your farts for hours.

Thrifty: You always keep a couple of good farts in reserve.

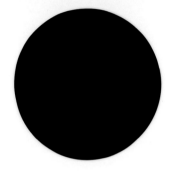

Anti-Social: When the need arises, you excuse yourself from the room and fart in private.

Strategic: You fart and then conceal it with loud coughing.

Intellectual: You can determine from the smell of any fart exactly what food item had been consumed.

Athletic: You fart at the slightest exertion.

Miserable: You would love to let one out, but you are unable to fart.

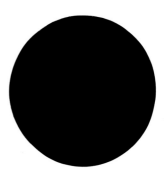

Sensitive: You fart and then start crying.

Fart Puns!

Romeo, Romeo, wherefore Fart thou Romeo?

Belly Laugh Fart Jokes for Kids

State of the Fart

Man after my own Fart

To my Fart's content

The Fartian

What Fart of no don't you understand?

Wear your Fart on your sleeve

ABu

The Fart of War

AAU

O Brother, Where Fart Thou?

AAU

Wild at Fart

AAU

Museum of Modern Fart

Home is where the Fart is

☆

Take his advice to Fart

☆

Church of the Sacred Fart

☆

Listen to your Fart

☆

Artificial Fart valve

☆

Anyone who can fart on command belongs in an insta toot.

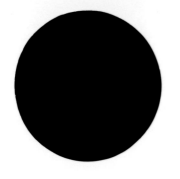

Shakespeare's play about surprisingly fragrant flatulence, aka *All Smells That Ends Well*.

If someone cries 'Fart!' in a crowded theatre, everyone must exit in an odorly fashion.

A husband was accused by his wife of farting. His plea: I no scent.

A Man After My Own Fart

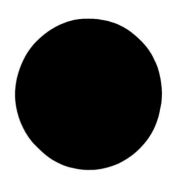

When dinosaurs lost the ability to fart, they faced ex-stinktion.

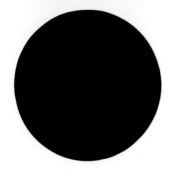

I am a professional flatulence-connoisseur. I enjoy fartisan whines.

I began owning up to my flatulence, after eating a frank-farter.

I farted in my wallet. Now I have gas money.

Mind if I hang out here until it's safe back where I farted?

Did you fart? 'cuz you just blew me away!

Who Farted?

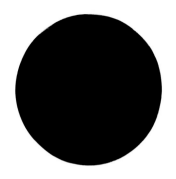

He who declared it blared it.

He who observed it served it.

He who detected it ejected it.

He who rejected it respected it.

He who said the rhyme did the crime.

Whoever spoke last set off the blast.

Whoever smelt it dealt it.

Whoever denied it supplied it.

He who snuffed it fluffed it

Types of Farts

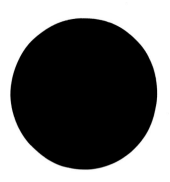

ARROGANT FART: "My farts don't stink"

CONFUSED FART: Gets lost on the way to your butt, and turns back and comes out your throat (a.k.a. burp)

ARTSY FART: A true work of art. Major points from the judges for smell, color, texture, and longevity.

BRAIN FART: You need to fart, but you suffer from a mental block.

GHOST FART: The ones you lay in your sleep that don't make a sound and don't smell.

HOME ALONE FART: The loud, smelly ones you lay in the comfort of your own home.

JAIL FART: Stuck inside you all day, then makes its escape as soon as you get home from work.

NOT ME FART: Releasing the hounds in public, and blaming it on someone else.

OLD FART: The kind Grandpa blames on you and gets away with.

TIRE FART: A real blow-out.

U.F.O. FART: When someone else releases a NOT ME FART.

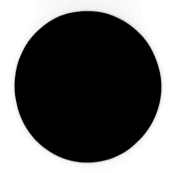

SHOE FART: You bend over to tie your shoelaces and oops!

Alternate Farts

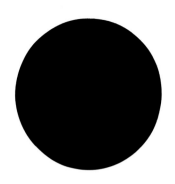

A message from Turd Castle.

Air biscuit

Air Jordan

Barked

Backstreet Boys

Barked beans

☆

Bean sprouts

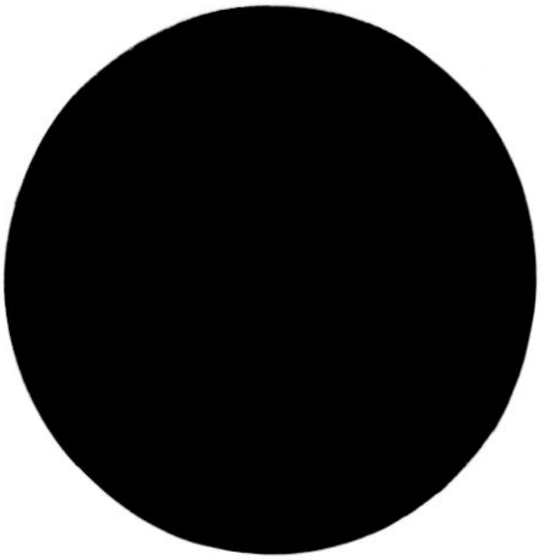

Bench warmer

☆

Bips

☆

Blast

☆

Blatt!

☆

Blow-Holes.

☆

Blowing mud.

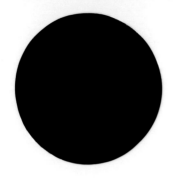

Blowing the butt trumpet.

Bottom burp

Butt burner

Cheesers

Clouds of chaos

Colon quack.

Cracking a rat.

Crack splitters.

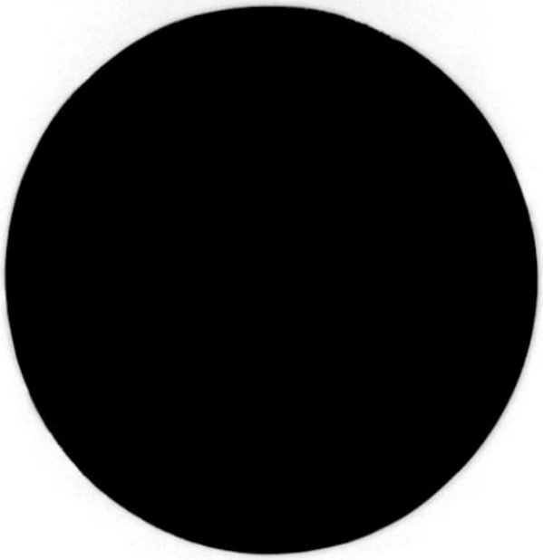

Cutting the cheese.

☆

Disappointments from down under.

☆

Draw mud.

☆

Dropped a shoe.

☆

Dropping your guts.

Escape from the planet of the gapes.

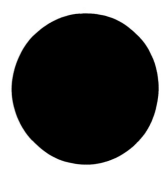

⭐

Flatulence

⭐

Fluff

⭐

Foul's Hoot

⭐

Gravy pants

Belly Laugh Fart Jokes for Kids

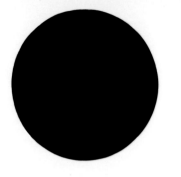

Grep

Guff

Happy honkers

Heinie burp

Hotties

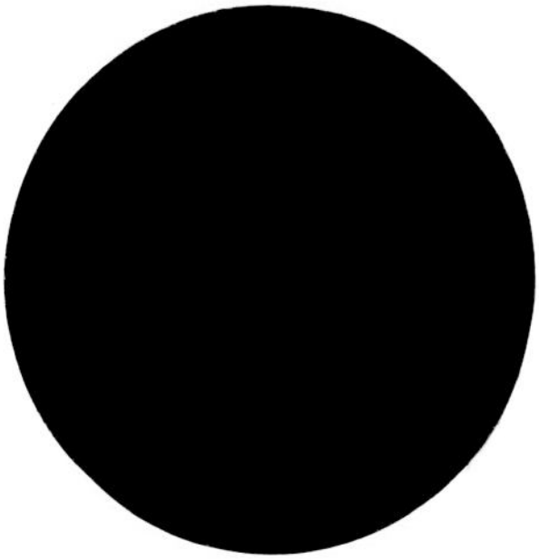

Belly Laugh Fart Jokes for Kids

Janet

☆

K-Fart

☆

Makin' beans

☆

Message from Uranus

☆

Mud crickets

Mud duck

My butt has something to say . . .

Natural Gas

Nature's little surprises

Nature's musical box

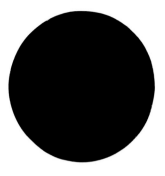

One turd honking at another for the right of way.

Ooh, that's a nasty cough

Oops, I let Fluffy off the leash!

Pant Burps

Parps

Phoofs

Belly Laugh Fart Jokes for Kids

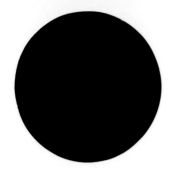

Pieru

☆

Poof

☆

Poots

☆

Pull my finger!

Quakers—9.5 on the Rectal Scale!

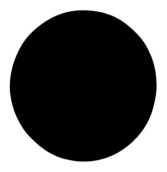

Rat Bark

Rosebuds

S.A.V. Silent And Violent

S.B.D. Silent But Deadly

Schnurs

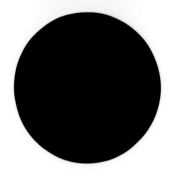

Shootin' bunnies

Short snort

Sidewinder

Silence in the court, my bums about to talk...

Smell-O-Gram

Speak to me ol' toothless wonder.

Belly Laugh Fart Jokes for Kids

Stinkies

☆

Thar she blows!

The Great Equalizer

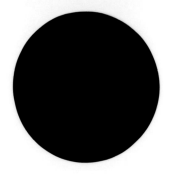

There goes a mouse on a motorcycle.

Thunder from down under.

Tooters

Tree frog

Trouser cough

Trouser ghost

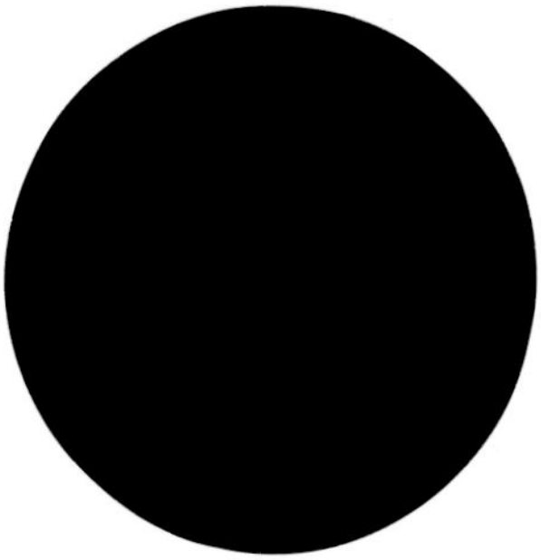

Trouser rippers

⭐

Trouser trumpet

⭐

Trump

⭐

Turd honking

⭐

Turd Tooties

⭐

Turds slamming on the brakes.

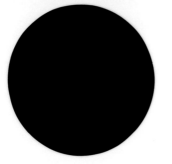

Underthunder

Who dropped their guts?

Who stepped on a duck?

Winds

Woofer

The Fart List

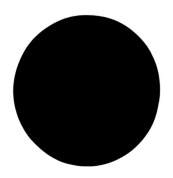

The Alarm Fart—Starts with a loud unnaturally high note, wavers like a siren, and ends with a quick downward note that stops before you expect it to. If it happens to you, will know right off why it is called the Alarm Fart. You will be alarmed.

The After Shower Fart—That unwanted fart that occurs right after you walk out of the shower feeling fresh and nice.

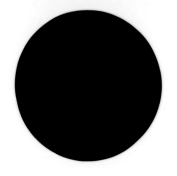

The Amplified Fart—This is any fart that gets its power more from being amplified than from the fart itself.

The Anticipated Fart—This one warns that it is back there waiting for some time before it arrives.

The Arrogant Fart—When the perpetrator thinks their farts don't stink.

The Atom Bomb Fart—The atom bomb fart is loud as heck, and it smells bad too. Also results in a big explosion, and everyone falls to the ground.

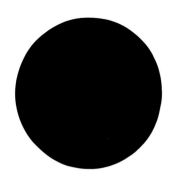

The Back Draft—The hollow, soul-rending fart that surprises even you.

The Back Seat Fart—This is a fart that occurs only in cars. The Back Seat Fart can usually be concealed by traffic noise as it is an eased-out fart and not very loud. But its foul odor will give it away, due to the way air moves around in a car. It is often followed by someone saying, "Who farted in the back seat?"

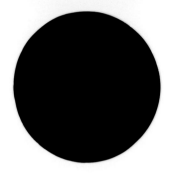

The Gutsy Fart—You're in a predicament where you would have to be gutsy in order to let it go . . .

The Banana Fart—A mostly silent fart that squeaks out an odorous gas that smells like a rotten smelly old banana.

The Bananana Fart—Same as above, but longer . . .

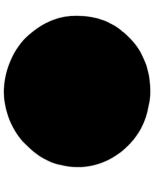

The Banshee—A high, keening wail that makes others uncomfortable.

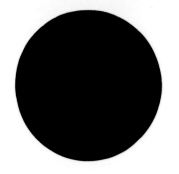

The Barking Spider Fart—A non-smelling fart which occurs in a crowded place. The farter cannot be identified and the sound is therefore blamed on a 'Barking Spider'.

The Barn Owl Fart—It's a sort of a crazy laugh, particularly the way it ends. If you hear a fart that has about eight notes in it, ending on a couple of down notes, and it sounds maniacal, you have heard the rare Barn Owl Fart.

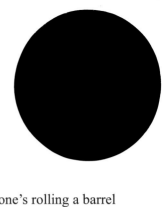

The Barrel Of Laughs Fart—
The kind of fart when you feel it coming a mile away, so you go and sit on your friend's lap and let her rip. Sounds like someone's rolling a barrel down your butthole.

☆

The Bathtub Fart—It is the only fart you can see! What you see is the bubbles.

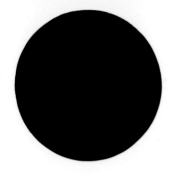

The Bear Fart (aka Nightmare On Smell Street)—The kind of fart that will wake you up at night because it smells so bad! They can be either silent or noisy—But they are the stinkiest farts imaginable!

The Beefy One—Sounds loud, and butch eg. 'BRAAAAMMPPP!'. Will smell a bit like the rotting offspring of cow and dog poop.

Belly Laugh Fart Jokes for Kids

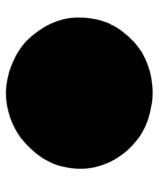

The Biggest Fart In The World Fart—Like the great bald eagle, this fart is pretty well described just by its name.

The Bitburr—Sounds like just that—you're walking and the initial explosion "BIT!" during one step is followed by a more gentle release of the rest of the volume during the next step: "brrrrrr . . ."

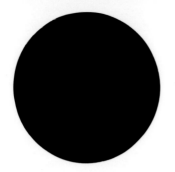

The Blame It On The Dog

Fart—The dog did it, not me.

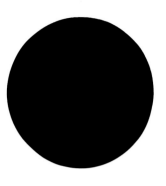

The Blind Date Fart—Happens while you are on a blind date or meeting new people. While getting to know each other, looking your best, and putting your best face forward –BRRAAMP.

The Breaking Dawn—A fart that wakes you up.

The Brewer Fart—You try to push a brewer fart the last furlong, but it stays firmly lodged deep within your bowels. You come to the conclusion that it is some form of gaseous landmark.

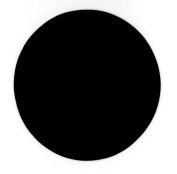

The Bubble Bobble Fart—This type of fart occurs while one is sitting. As one sits down, a gaseous bubble fart pokes out just a little bit under one's butt to cause a rocking sensation, as if one is sitting on a beach ball.

The Bubble Fart—You feel it at the edge of your butt and you think that it is gone but then it pops and is one of the most smelliest farts possible.

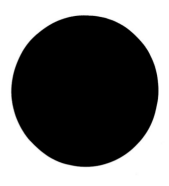

The Bubble Gum Fart—A bubbly but wet fart that smells so horribly bad you don't even enjoy it.

The Bubble Wrap Fart—Farted by people who sit a lot during the day. Known for it's bubble wrap popping sound effect, which is similar to a machine gun, but much duller.

The Buddah—This fart is the mother of all farts. It starts out like a car's engine, vroom vroom, and then it backfires (*BOOM*) and it knocks the family cat a couple of miles.

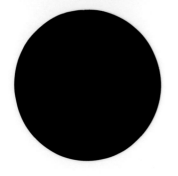

The Bullet Fart—Its single and most pronounced diagnostic characteristic is its sound. It sounds like a rifle shot. It can startle spectators and farter alike.

The Bunbuster Fart—Sounds like a Beefy One, except much more sudden and much much more powerful. Generally smells eggy or beefy.

The Burning Brakes Fart—The Burning Brakes Fart actually does smell a little like burning brakes, and seems to hang around longer than most farts, which gives whoever farted a chance to make a big show of checking to see if the emergency brake has been left on.

The Burp 'N' Fart—It's when you burp and fart at the same time.

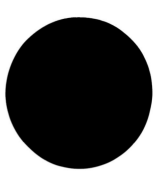

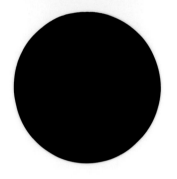

The Butt Rocket Fart—This scary but predictable fart is provoked by eating large quantities of fast food at one sitting. It doesn't make any appreciable noise until it is just about through.

The Buttripper Fart—The kind that comes out so fast and hard that it rips your cheeks apart and makes you cry. And it smells horribly too.

The Camo-Fart—If you're sitting in class one day and suddenly a little squeak pops out, if someone asks you if you farted, be sure that your desk is tuned properly so that it may squeak at the same frequency as your fart. Then tell the person that it was your desk.

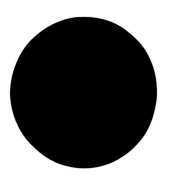

The Car Door Fart—Either a group one or a group two fart. Very tricky. A matter of close timing is involved, the farter trying to fart at the exact moment he slams the car door shut. It is usually a good loud fart. It is one of the funnier farts when it doesn't work, which is almost every time.

The Cat's Meow Fart—Sounds like slowly dying cat and lasts roughly 7.5 seconds. Also, the wrinkled grin/face of agony has to accompany it.

Belly Laugh Fart Jokes for Kids

The Celestial Fart—The Celestial Fart is soft and delicate, surprising in a boy or an adult.

The Church Hymn Fart—The kind where you're sitting in church, you bend over to pick up a hymn book, and -PBBBBBBT!!!- a giant fart rips out.

The Command Fart—Can be held for long periods of time waiting for the right moment. It is intended to be noticed.

The Common Fart—This fart needs little description. It is to the world of farts what the house sparrow is to the world of birds.

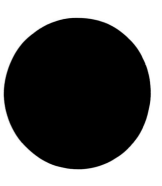

The Compost Fart—You know the compost heap that a gardener keeps at the bottom of the garden? Well if you jump on it you will have some idea of what a compost fart sounds and smells like. Do not attempt this one while you have company.

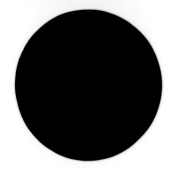

The Computer Fart—The kind where you are playing on the computer, and it just slips out.

The Crop Duster—You walk past a person, group, or crowd and silently fart, so they can smell it and think someone else did it. Basically, it is defined as farting while walking.

The Crowd Fart—The Crowd Fart is distinguished by its very potent odor, strong enough to make quite a few people look around. The trick here is not to identify the fart but the farter.

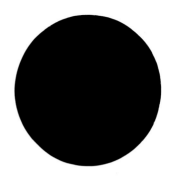

The Cushioned Fart—A concealed fart, sometimes successful. They will squirm and push their butt way down into the cushions of a sofa or over-stuffed chair and ease-out a fart very carefully without moving then or for some time after. Some odor may escape, but usually not much.

The Delayed Reaction Fart—You have the urge, but it goes away. You go on about your business and a few seconds, or longer, later, 'BBRRMMPHH'. . .

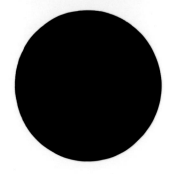

The Did An Angel Speak Fart—This is any loud fart in church.

The Didgeridoo Fart—Only emitted after some sort of surgery. The result of gas and air trapped in the body during the procedure. They are long, loud, and alternate in notes. Often exaggerated when the farter laughs.

The Dog Whistle Fart—You can't hear it, but someone is going to know it's there.

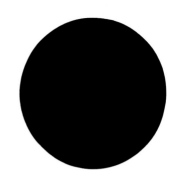

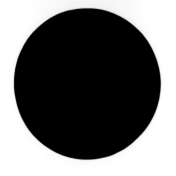

The Dud Fart—A fart that fails. It is the most private of all farts, and most of the time the farter feels a little disappointed.

The Echo Fart—The true Echo Fart is a fart that makes its own echo. It is a two-toned fart, the first tone loud, then a pause, and then the second tone.

The Eggy Fart—Smells very much like rotten eggs. A powerful odor which tends to put people off lunch. Often rips out in the fashion of a Bunbuster.

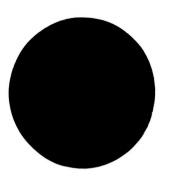

The Escape Pod Fart—You think you got away with this one. You forced it out as silently as possible, and nobody heard. You take deep sniffs through your nose, as discreetly as possible. You smell nothing but your deodorant. Then 30 seconds later, as if released from a stasis field, everyone starts to cough and splutter.

The Electrical Fart—Sounds like they have some juice in them.

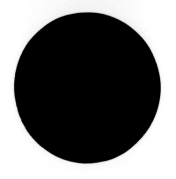

The Exploding Mouse Fart—While trying to hold it in, some gas gets out making a squeak noise, and since relieving yourself a little bit felt so good, you let the rest out in a huge BRAP!

The Flapping Flutter Fart—This one's an earth shaker, but not too deadly on the odor side. It's distinguished by its long and loud flutter sound, and its marked vibrations are felt by all who are on the same bed or sofa.

The Flatus—A stately fart. If it were a person it would wear a monocle.

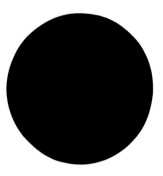

The Floral Flatulence—They are very unique, and to the expulsion expert they are among the most pleasant scented. Some have often tried to bottle this scent, but it cannot be captured.

The Flutterbuster Fart—Farting whilst seated on a vinyl covered surface.

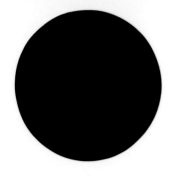

The Foggy Window Fart—You're sitting in the car at night or early in the morning, and after some time of getting the windows defogged, someone has to fart and fog the windows backup.

The G and L Fart—This is one of the most ordinary and pedestrian of farts, known to everyone. Certainly it is the least gross. G and L stands for Gambled and Lost. One of the most embarrassing of all farts, even when you are alone.

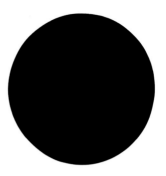

The Ghost Of Dinners Past— Smells of what you ate a good three meals ago.

The Ghost Fart—A doubtful fart in most cases, as it is supposed to be identified by odor alone and to occur, for instance, in an empty house. You enter and smell a fart, yet no one is there.

The Glad It Wasn't Mine Fart—So nasty in smell, odor, and sound, that you have to thank God it didn't come from your behind.

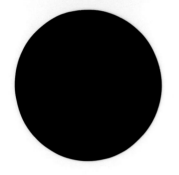

The Gobble Fart—Sounds like a turkey gobbling . . .

The Greetings! Fart—You let one rip as a greeting or a way to say, "Hi!"

The Growling Fart—Happens deep within the rectum (and therefore has no smell). Somehow never meets the light of day. Tends to growl like a dog at the vets.

The Gunshot Fart—Gunshot farts sound just like a gunshot.

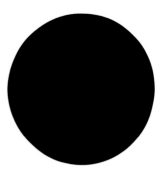

The Had To Poop But Only Farted Fart—You run to the bathroom with the urge to purge and you let her rip, only to find that you had a huge fart.

The Harmonica Fart—Usually short, high pitched, in a series of notes. If strained, they have been known to bend and change. And sometimes the small ones get sucked back in.

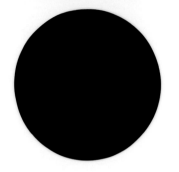

The Hay Fever Fart—You fart at the same time that you sneeze.

The Hic-Hachoo-Fart—This is strictly an old lady's fart. What happens is that the person manages to hiccup, sneeze, and fart all at the same time. There is no reason she should not be proud, as this is probably as neat an old person's fart as there is.

The Home Alone Fart—A loud, smelly one you lay in the comfort of your own home.

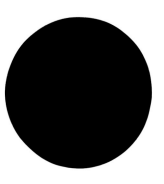

The Horror Movie Scare Fart—You're watching a horror movie and by either suspense or fright, you let one rip.

The Independence Day Fart—Such an explosive whopper that it sends everyone screaming out of the area.

The Interrogative Fart—Starts out low, and rises in pitch towards its conclusion. Sounds like your butt is asking a question.

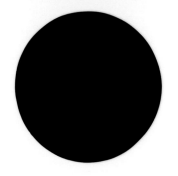

The It's Stuck! Fart—Usually a timid fart (not much air) while you're sitting down, but when you let it out, it sticks between the cheeks as a tiny air bubble.

The Jail Fart—Been doing time inside you for quite awhile and releasing it would be a crime.

The Jerk Fart—The Jerk Fart is a fart by a jerk who smirks, smiles, grins, and points to himself in case you missed it. It is usually a single-noted, off-key, fading away, sort of whistle fart, altogether pitiful, but the jerk will act as if he has just farted the Biggest Fart in the World Fart.

Belly Laugh Fart Jokes for Kids

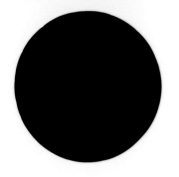

The John Fart—Any ordinary fart farted on the toilet. If it is all the person's trip to the john amounted to, he will be disappointed for sure.

The Kettle Drum Fart—Beats hard against your chair to emit a low, reverberating, rumbling sound.

The Kweeeeef Fart—Sitting in band class with perfect posture when you let a fart that sounds like a squeaking clarinet.

Belly Laugh Fart Jokes for Kids

The Laughing Fart—When you are laughing so hard at something you fart, and you can't deny it because everyone heard it and you might as well admit your guilt.

The Lead Fart—The heaviest of all farts. It sounds like a dropped ripe watermelon. Or a falling body in some cases. It is the only fart that goes thud.

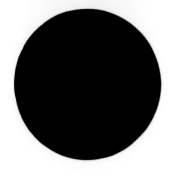

The Lonely Fart—This is the type you do when you're on your own, so you don't care about the smell or the noise.

The Loud And Deadly Fart—Like the silent but deadly fart—except it is heard by everyone, and it will cause people to faint.

The Malted Milk Ball Fart—Odor alone is diagnostic and positively identifies this fart. It smells exactly like malted milk balls.

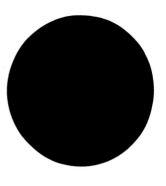

The Mario's Jump Fart—Named after the famous and acclaimed Mario Jump, which, well, . . . you know . . . sounds like Mario's Jump -TOUUNG.

The Taco Fart—The one that reminds you of the taco you had the night before and it makes you hungry.

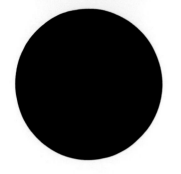

The Migrating Fart—This fart sneaks out of your butt and remains there feeling about the size of a walnut or small tomato. It is when you sit up in a more erect posture that you feel it inch its way upward and then apparently dissipates somewhere behind your back or perhaps inside your shirt.

The Morning Fart—The first thing out of bed fart. Long, loud, and not too smelly.

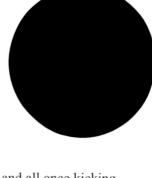

The Mothball Fart—Noted for coming from elderly folks—usually in a casual manner with little to no noise. But when the scent is out—it reeks of mothballs and all once kicking bugs fall limp to the ground . . .

The Motor Boat Fart—Starts with a modest "put", then follows up with a series that sounds like someone firing up an outboard motor and speeding off across the lake.

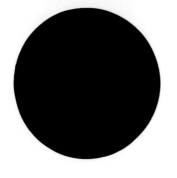

The Motorcycle Fart—When someone is riding on the back of your motorcycle and you fart, they can usually smell them.

The Mouth Fart—Comes out the other end but you couldn't tell by the smell.

The Movie Theater Fart—You are sitting in a movie theater and you have to let one go, so you wait for an opening, such as a big explosion, to let it go.

The Musical Fart—This is most common with elders entertaining small children. The fart is performed by first setting up the incident with a musical beginning, such as "I'm Popeye the Sailor Man." Toot-Toot. The toots are replaced with the musical fart.

The Never Ending Fart—This is the fart that doesn't end . . . Yes it goes on and on my friends . . .

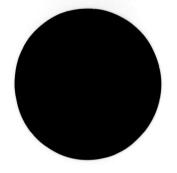

The Nonchalant Fart—The fart is very audible yet the farter just continues with whatever activity or conversation he or she happened to be engaged in as if it had never happened. It makes you wonder if they actually realized they did it.

The Not Now!—You feel the presence of a mighty fart, but are unable to release it due to your situation. Success depends on a number of factors, but it's usually a game you can't win.

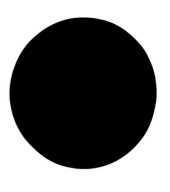

The Oh My God Fart—This is the most awful and dreadful stinking of all farts—a fart that smells like a month-old rotten egg.

The On The Spot Fart—You didn't even know it was there, but suddenly "Brrmp".

The One Cheek Sneak Fart—This fart happens when you put your weight on one butt cheek and lift the other up.

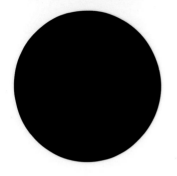

The Organic Fart—Sometimes called the Health Food Nut Fart. The person who farts an Organic Fart may be talking about the healthy food he eats even when he farts.

The Phish Fart—When this bad biscuit erupts, it has a catch of the day scent.

Belly Laugh Fart Jokes for Kids

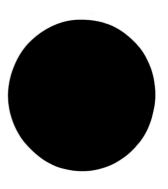

The Piggyback Fart—Only occurs in those situations where it would be a "personal disaster" to fart (e.g. crowded room, business meeting). You are holding onto this bad boy for dear life when suddenly someone else drops a LOUD one. Before the noise of this one has finished you let one rip as fast a possible so both farts sound as one.

The Plain Jane—One-second duration, nice resonant reverberation, and pungent odor cloud with a nearly instantaneous 5-foot radius. Your standard, everyday, friendly fart.

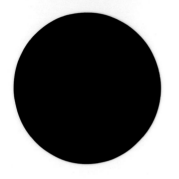

The Point Blank Fart—A prank done on a unsuspecting victim by pointing it toward the victim's face. This is successfully accomplished when the victim is sleeping or watching TV.

The Polite Fart—You feel the urge and excuse yourself to the other room where you politely let it rip.

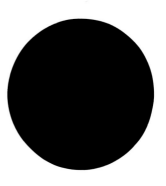

The Predator Fart—This fart seems to actually seek out a victim after leaving its maker. Usually an innocent friend in the back seat of the car or a couple of seats away in a theater. The predator fart will skip over others and wrap itself around its victim with a vicious fury.

The Prorr-Wooort Fart—That's the nice, long, modulated sound it makes.

Belly Laugh Fart Jokes for Kids

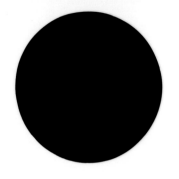

The Pull My Finger Fart— You ask someone to pull your finger when you feel a big gassy fart come. After they pull your finger, you fart.

The Pumpkin Fart—A warm, dry, fart that smells like an old Jack-O-Lantern. An aroma pleasing to the creator, but one which will clear a large room.

The Quiver Fart—When you fart, it quivers. If it tickles, then it is the Tickle Fart.

The Really Good Fake Fart—Someone make a noise that sounds like a fart and blames it on you or someone else.

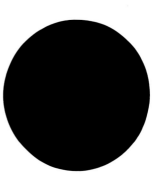

The Relief Fart—Sound or odor don't matter on this one. What matters is the tremendous sense of relief that you have finally farted. Some people will even say, "Wow, what a relief."

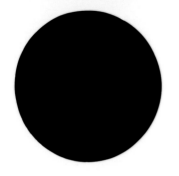

The Reluctant Fart—Probably one of the oldest farts known to man, it is a fart that seems to have a mind of its own. It will come when it is ready, not before. This can take half a day in some instances.

The Rusty Gate Fart—The sound of this fart seems almost impossible for a fart. It is the most dry and squeaky sound a fart can make.

The Sandpaper Fart—This one scratches. Otherwise it may not amount to much. You should remember that if you reach back and scratch, it automatically becomes a Scratch Fart.

The Shaking Fart—The one you get during class or a meeting and holding it in makes your body convulse.

The Show Off Fart—A fart that you purposely give off to show what a loud smelly one you can make.

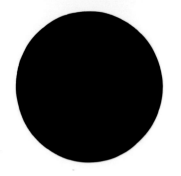

The Silent But Deadly (SBD) Fart—The type that remains totally inaudible, yet somehow causes all the occupants of a room to collapse. Can smell like anything - nasal investigators rarely have time to distinguish an odor.

The Silent But Violent Fart— This type of fart is not heard, but will cause facial hair to disintegrate, nasal passages to blister from the burn, eyes to water, and nausea.

The Silent . . . But Eggy Fart—The kind of fart you do when you're with a crowd. It is silent, but smells like a rotten egg.

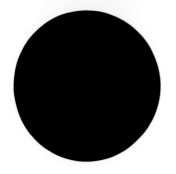

The Sitting High Jump Fart—The fart you unleash on the toilet when you need to get it out in a hurry. Mostly happens in public restrooms when you believe the bathroom is empty but may become occupied at any moment. Named for the rocket-propulsion action of the odor cloud.

The Small Fart—It's the kind of fart where you just hear a "beep".

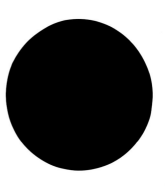

The Snart—This is a fart that you succeed in suppressing so as not to not to offend, but then a sneeze jars it loose.

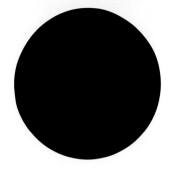

The Sonic Boom Fart—The people who believe in this fart claim it is even bigger than the Biggest Fart In The World Fart. The Sonic Boom Fart is supposed to shake the house and rattle the windows.

The Squeaky Fart—Sounds like "Wheeek". Normally smells foul.

The Staged Fart—This little number comes out in small bursts of the same length.

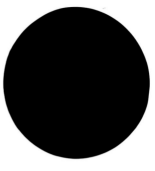

The Stalker Fart—Occurs when you leave the room to politely fart elsewhere, and save people the trouble of smelling it. You go back into the room, but LO! The odor has followed you.

The Stay Awhile Fart—The one you let rip in bed a couple of nights ago, that is still there and smells even worse.

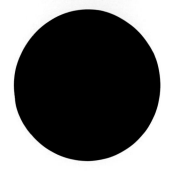

The Stealth Fart—A stealth fart is similar to the Point Blank fart but uses the Silent But Deadly Fart. Just when you're ready to release your SBD, you would walk toward a group of guests and then release your payload and slowly walk away. Then the guests won't know what hit them.

The Stolen Fart—Someone else lets it, but it's so good that you claim it.

The Subterranean Yawn—A long, drawn out fart that keeps going after the sound dies off.

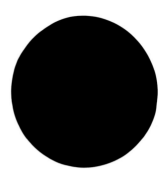

The Synchronous Fart—More than one person farts in sync. Sounds neat.

The Tandem Fart—They are so named since they are the only fart that is detectable by the nose on a tandem bicycle (bicycle built for two). A tandem fart occurs when the captain of the bike farts and the stoker smells it.

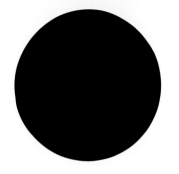

The Teflon Fart—Slips out without a sound and no strain at all. A very good fart in situations where you would rather not fart at all. You can be talking to someone and not miss saying a word. If the wind is right they will never know.

The Tension Breaker Fart—Usually during a test or some stressful meeting where everyone is concentrating, and someone in the room lets a fart that, rather than making people gag, makes everyone laugh. Then of course, if it was at school, people start imitating it.

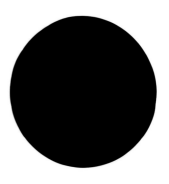

The Thank God I'm Alone Fart—Everyone knows this rotten fart. You look around after you have farted and say, "Thank God I'm alone." Then you get out of there fast.

The Tickle Fart—Usually a slow, soft sort of fart. If you like being tickled, this is the fart for you.

The Timid Fart—Short, sweet, petite, not much odor, and not much air.

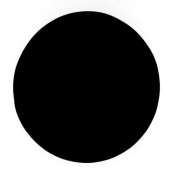

The Triple Flutter Blast—To properly "perform" it, one leg must be elevated and resting on a convenient chair or stool. It happens in three short but powerful bursts.

The Trombone Fart—Starts out low and then slides upward to a higher pitch.

The Trumpet Fart—High pitched, with a staccato quality. Quite brassy.

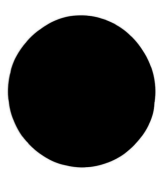

The Tuba Fart—Loud and low-pitched.

The Twist-Of-Fate Dog Fart—The dog lets a fart so big that everyone blames it on you.

The UFO Fart—Stands for "Unidentified Foul Odor". When someone farts in crowded room, but nobody knows what the rotten smell is.

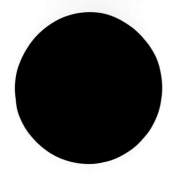

The Underwear Ripper Fart—It is one of the longer farts, and will sound so much like a piece of cloth being ripped that it can fool a person sitting in the next room. Naturally it will not fool the farter.

The Uptight Fart—When the person knows he has to fart, like it or not, and he gets even more uptight. Squeak, squeak, squeak.

The Ventriloquist Fart—This is something that just happens. It is doubtful if anyone can learn to throw his farts. But sometimes, if all the conditions are right, it will happen.

The Vibrating Fart—The person sitting next to you can feel it.

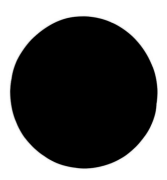

The Waker-Upper Fart—The first fart of the morning.

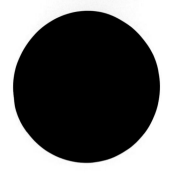

The Walking Fart—The kind that makes a little sound every time you take a step.

The Who Cut The Cheese Fart—Someone has got to say "Who cut the cheese?" when the fart is first noticed or it cannot be called a Who Cut The Cheese Fart.

The Windy Fart—The sort of fart which goes "Whoosh", and is more felt than heard. A little like an SBD, but louder and considerably less toxic.

The Yo-Yo Fart—This is a spectacular fart. A real dilly. It starts out on the highest fart note possible and goes all the way down to the lowest fart note possible. And then, to the amazement of everyone, it comes all the way back up again. Extremely rare.

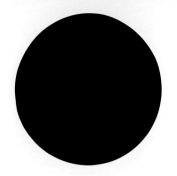

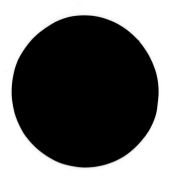